# The A–Z of Minding Me

For my daughter, Callie, and children everywhere.
Thank you for inspiring me.

TRACEY

For David, Poppi, Seb and Holly with love.

NIAMH

# The A–Z of Minding Me

Tracey Flynn and Niamh Gogan

ILLUSTRATED BY
Kerry O'Callaghan

GILL BOOKS

I can …

# Adapt

to change and try
new things.

I can …

# Breathe

long and slow to calm
my busy mind.

I can …

# Cry

and be comforted by
someone I trust.

I can …

# Dream

and dare to be different.

I can …

# Exercise

and keep my body healthy.

# I can … Feel

lots of different emotions,
and know my feelings
come and go.

I can … **Giggle**

and be happy.

I can …

# Hug

myself, my teddy or a friend.

# I can … Invent

and use my imagination to
create and explore.

I can … Jiggle

to my own groove.

I can …

# Know

kindness is a gift I give and receive.

I can …

# Love

myself, anyone or anything.

I can … **Mind**

myself and others by being safe and kind.

I can …

# Nurture

nature, animals and bugs.

I can …

# Overcome

difficult moments and be okay.

I can …

# Play

and learn in
different ways every day.

I can …

# Question

and wonder why.

I can …

# Respect

my body, my belongings and others.

I can …

# Sense

all the incredible
things around me.

I can …

# Think

about what makes
me happy and say
'thank you'.

I can say …

# ‘Uh-oh!’

when I make a mistake.

I can …

# Voice

how I feel and be
seen and heard.

I can …

# Wow

and be wonderful
just by being me.

I can …

# eXpress

who I am, in any way I like.

I can say …

# ‘Yippee’

when positive things
happen for me.

I can …

# Zzzzzz

rest, recharge and know…

I'm minding me.

**Tracey Flynn** is a mum and primary school teacher. She holds a master's degree in Dramatherapy and is accredited in Children's Mindfulness Practice.

**Niamh Gogan** lives in Dublin with her husband, David, and their two children, Poppi and Seb, and she is stepmum to Holly. She holds an honours degree in Psychology, is accredited in Therapeutic Play Skills and is currently undertaking an MA in Creative Psychology.

**Kerry O'Callaghan** is an illustrator and designer from Kinsale, Co. Cork. She holds a BA in Graphic Design from Limerick School of Art and Design, and an MA in Children's Book Illustration from Cambridge School of Art.

Gill Books
Hume Avenue
Park West
Dublin 12
www.gillbooks.ie

Gill Books is an imprint of M.H. Gill and Co.



978 07171 9429 2

Designed by Graham Thew
Printed and bound by Hussar Books, Poland
This book is typeset in Bembo Std 26pt.

The paper used in this book comes from the wood pulp of sustainably managed forests.



A CIP catalogue record for this book is available from the British Library.

5 4 3 2 1